CW00430258

This book belongs to

LOOK OUT FOR MORE
COLORING BOOKS
FROM BEAM COLORS

FLOWER PATTERNS COLORING BOOK 1

FLOWER PATTERNS COLORING BOOK 1

FLOWER PATTERNS COLORING BOOK 1

FLOWER PATTERNS COLORING BOOK 1

FLOWER PATTERNS COLORING BOOK 1

FLOWER PATTERNS COLORING BOOK 1

FLOWER PATTERNS COLORING BOOK 1

FLOWER PATTERNS COLORING BOOK 1

FLOWER PATTERNS COLORING BOOK 1

FLOWER PATTERNS COLORING BOOK 1

FLOWER PATTERNS COLORING BOOK 1

FLOWER PATTERNS COLORING BOOK 1

FLOWER PATTERNS COLORING BOOK 1

FLOWER PATTERNS COLORING BOOK 1

FLOWER PATTERNS COLORING BOOK 1

FLOWER PATTERNS COLORING BOOK 1

FLOWER PATTERNS COLORING BOOK 1

FLOWER PATTERNS COLORING BOOK 1

FLOWER PATTERNS COLORING BOOK 1

FLOWER PATTERNS COLORING BOOK 1

FLOWER PATTERNS COLORING BOOK 1

FLOWER PATTERNS COLORING BOOK 1

FLOWER PATTERNS COLORING BOOK 1

FLOWER PATTERNS COLORING BOOK 1

FLOWER PATTERNS COLORING BOOK 1

FLOWER PATTERNS COLORING BOOK 1

FLOWER PATTERNS COLORING BOOK 1

FLOWER PATTERNS COLORING BOOK 1

FLOWER PATTERNS COLORING BOOK 1

FLOWER PATTERNS COLORING BOOK 1

FLOWER PATTERNS COLORING BOOK 1

FLOWER PATTERNS COLORING BOOK 1

FLOWER PATTERNS COLORING BOOK 1

FLOWER PATTERNS COLORING BOOK 1

FLOWER PATTERNS COLORING BOOK 1

FLOWER PATTERNS COLORING BOOK 1

FLOWER PATTERNS COLORING BOOK 1

FLOWER PATTERNS COLORING BOOK 1

FLOWER PATTERNS COLORING BOOK 1

FLOWER PATTERNS COLORING BOOK 1

FLOWER PATTERNS COLORING BOOK 1

FLOWER PATTERNS COLORING BOOK 1

FLOWER PATTERNS COLORING BOOK 1

FLOWER PATTERNS COLORING BOOK 1

FLOWER PATTERNS COLORING BOOK 1

FLOWER PATTERNS COLORING BOOK 1

FLOWER PATTERNS COLORING BOOK 1

FLOWER PATTERNS COLORING BOOK 1

FLOWER PATTERNS COLORING BOOK 1

FLOWER PATTERNS COLORING BOOK 1

LOOK OUT FOR MORE
COLORING BOOKS
FROM BEAM COLORS

Printed in Great Britain
by Amazon